THE **PINEAPPLE STORY**

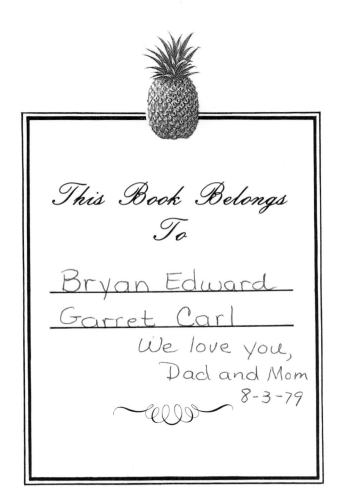

This Book Belongs
To

Bryan Edward
Garret Carl
We love you,
Dad and Mom
8-3-79

Printed in the United States of America by
Rand McNally and Company

Library of Congress
Catalog Card Number: 78-60645

ISBN 0-916888-03-7

THE
PINEAPPLE STORY

INSTITUTE IN BASIC YOUTH CONFLICTS   •   OAK BROOK, ILLINOIS   •   U.S.A.

The pineapple story took place in Dutch New Guinea. It covered a period of seven years. It is a humorous yet profound illustration of applying a basic Scriptural principle.

As you read this first-hand account, you will discover that it is a classic example of the kinds of struggles which each of us faces until we learn and apply the principle of yielding personal rights.

$\mathcal{M}$y family and I work with these people way back in the bush.

One day I decided that I was going to bring in some pineapples.

The people had heard of pineapples. They had tasted them, but they didn't have any source to get them.

*S*o I got them from another mission station. I got about one hundred plants.

Then I got one of the local men to work for me. He planted all these pineapple shoots for me.

I paid him, of course. I paid him salt or whatever he wanted for the days he worked.

It seemed to take awfully long for those little shoots of pineapple to become big bushes and finally yield pineapples. It took about three years.

Back in the jungle you long for fresh fruit. You don't get much fresh fruit or vegetables.

*S*o finally that third year we could see fresh pineapples coming on, and we were just waiting for
Christmas time because that is when they are ripe.

When Christmas finally came, my wife and I would go
for walks to see if any were ripe enough to eat.

Finally, when they got ripe, we didn't get a single one of them! The natives stole every one!

They stole them before they were ripe. That is their art. Steal it before it is ripe or the owner gets it.

Here I am, a missionary, getting mad at these people.

Missionaries aren't supposed to get mad. You all know that. But I got angry.

I said, "Look, you guys! I have been waiting for these pineapples for three years. I didn't get any of them.

"Now there are others getting ripe. If any more of these pineapples are stolen, no more clinic for you."

$\mathcal{M}$y wife was running a clinic. She was giving them all their pills free. They didn't have anything to pay.

We were knocking ourselves out trying to help these people, taking care of their sick, saving the lives of their babies.

One by one the pineapples got ripe, and one by one they were stolen.

So I felt I had to stand my ground with these people. I couldn't just let them run all over me.

But that was not really the reason. It was a selfish reason. I wanted to eat those pineapples.

So no more clinic.

Then they let their sick babies die. They couldn't care less. Life was cheap over there. People with bad pneumonia would be coughing and begging us for medicine.

We would say, "No! Remember you stole our pineapples."

"I didn't steal them," they would say. "It was the other guys that did it."

They would go on coughing and begging. We couldn't take it any longer. I broke down and said, "Okay, tomorrow morning we will open the clinic again."

When we opened the clinic they started stealing the pineapples, and I felt bad again.

Man! These rascals!

*B*ut finally we found out who was doing it—the guy who had planted them.

I called him on the carpet and said, "Look, buddy! What are you doing stealing my pineapples? You are my gardener."

He said, "My hands plant them. My mouth eats them."
That is the rule of the jungle.

If they plant something, that is theirs. They had never
heard of the idea of paying for services.

So he said, "They are all mine."

I said, "Oh no! They are mine. I paid you to plant
them." But he just couldn't understand how that made
them my plants.

I thought, "Well, what do I do now? It was the rule of
their tribe. I'd better learn to live by their rule."

*S*o I said, "Alright, I will give you half of these plants.

"Everything from here to over there is yours. If they get ripe, they are yours. And these are mine."

He sounded like he was in agreement. But my pineapples still got stolen.

Then I thought, "Maybe I should let them have all those pineapples, and I'll get some new ones."

But I knew that I would have to wait three more years. That was hard for me to do.

Finally I said, "Look, I will give you all these pineapples, and then I will start all over again.

"Now you make a garden and you take all these pineapples out of my garden so I will have room to plant new ones. I don't want your pineapples in my garden if you feel they are yours."

So they said, "Too-wan, (which means outsider, foreigner) you will have to pay us."

I said, "Now, look!" They said, "No, no! You are asking us to move your pineapple bushes, and that is work."

Now they are mine. I said, "Alright, I'll pay you one day's work. Take them all away."

Then they said, "We don't have a garden ready. Will you pay us to get it ready?"

I said, "Forget it!" I was so fed up with them.

I told my wife, "This is impossible! I am just going to pay some guy to root them all out and throw them on the trash heap. Then if they want them they can just take them."

So we did. We rooted them all out and threw them on a heap. That was hard to do. They were nice pineapple bushes.

Then I bought new plants.

I *said, "Now look, all you guys. I am going to pay you to plant them, but I eat them, me and my family. You don't eat any."*

They said, "You can't do that. If we plant them, we eat them."

I said, "Look, I don't have time to mess with a garden. I have too much to do. There are so many of you, and there is only one me. You have got to help me. I want you to plant them, and I will eat them."

I said, "I will pay you. What do you want? I will give you this nice knife if you will agree to do it."

They started to think. "He will pay us that knife so he can eat our pineapples."

Finally they agreed.

During the next three years I reminded the guy who planted them, "Look! Who is going to eat these pineapples?"

He said, "You are."

I said, "Fine! Have you still got the knife?"

He said, "Yes."

I said, "Well, take good care of it."

If he lost the knife I am in trouble again. The pay is gone.

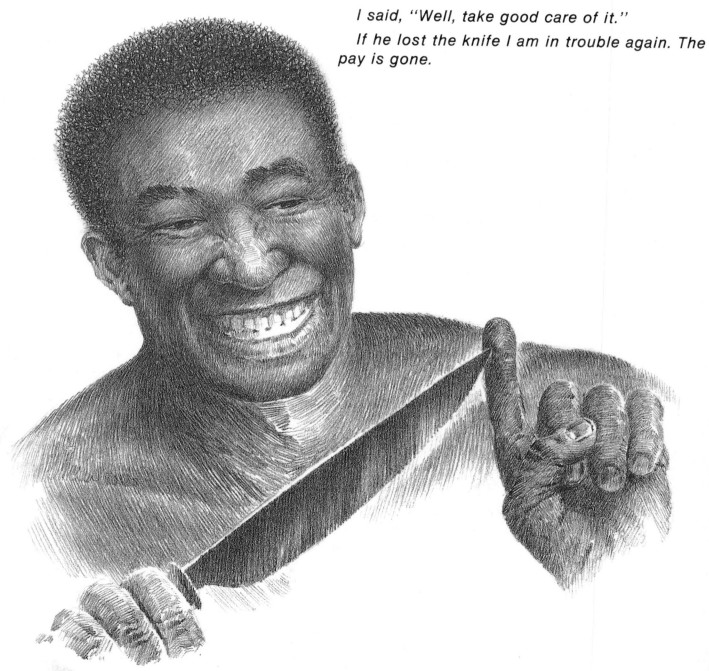

inally, after three more years the pineapples began to ripen.

My wife and I walked through the garden again. I said, "Man! Pretty soon we are going to have a crop of our own pineapples."

We started to thank God that He was providing them for us. But do you know what happened? Every one of them was stolen!

I would see the natives go through the garden in the daytime to spot where the pineapples were, and then at night they would be able to go right to them.

I thought, "What am I going to do? We can't cut out the clinic. Let's cut out the trade store."

That's where they get their matches, salt, fish hooks, and things like that. They used to do without them. That won't kill them.

I said, "Okay, no more store. You stole my pineapples."

When we closed the store they began to say, "We had better leave because we don't have any salt. If he is not going to have a store, there is no advantage for us being here with him. We might as well go back to our jungle houses."

So they took off to live in the jungle.

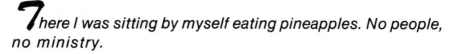

There I was sitting by myself eating pineapples. No people, no ministry.

I said to my wife, "Look, we can eat pineapples back in the States, I mean, if that is all we are here to do."

A runner returned and I said, "Get them all back. We will open the store next Monday."

I thought and thought. How am I going to get to eat those pineapples? There must be a way. Then I got an idea.

A German shepherd! I got the biggest German shepherd I could get on the island. I brought him in there and let him loose.

They were afraid of him. They had never seen a dog that big. They had little, mangy dogs. They never fed them. They were all diseased.

And there was this well-fed German shepherd dog.

They looked at the food he got. I would always have to feed him when the people weren't around because they would resent the dog's food. It was better than anything they got.

*B*ut that dog did the trick. Most of the people didn't dare come around anymore. So now we had the same result as closing the store.

People didn't come.

I didn't have anybody to talk to.

I couldn't get anybody to teach me the language.

I thought, "What do we do?"

The dog wasn't working. But in the meantime, the dog was starting to breed with the village dogs and would raise up a wicked half-shepherd, wild and hungry.

The doctor said, "Look! If your kids or anybody gets bitten by that dog, I am not going to treat them."

He was using the same tactics on me that I was using on the natives.

I said to my wife, "We've got to get rid of the dog."

Well, I got rid of the dog. I hated to do it.

$\mathcal{N}$ow the dog was gone. The people came back and no more pineapples.

I thought, "Boy! There must be a way. What can I do?"

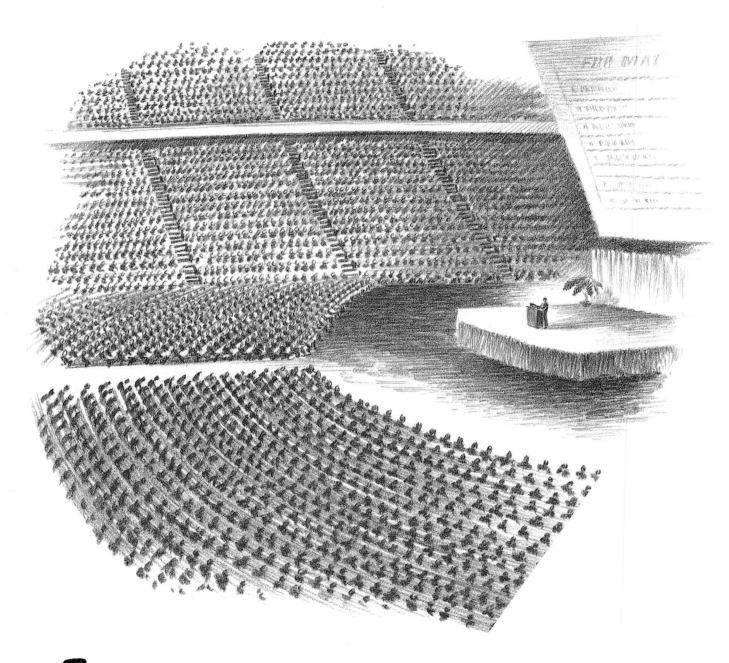

*T*hen I came home on furlough and went to a Basic Youth Seminar. I learned that we must give everything we own to God.

The Bible says if you give, you will have; if you keep for yourself, you will lose. Give your things to God, and God will see that you have enough.

This is a basic principle.

I thought, "Man! I don't have anything to lose. I will give that pineapple garden to God because I am not eating the pineapples anyway."

Now I know that is not a very good sacrifice. You are supposed to sacrifice something that is valuable to you.

But I would give it to God and see if He could control it.

I said, "Man! I am going to see how He is going to do it."

So I stood out in the garden one night. The people had gone home. I didn't want them to see me out there praying.

I prayed, "Lord, see these pineapple bushes? I have fought to have fruit from them. I have claimed them. I have stood up for my rights.

"It is all wrong, and I realize it now. I have seen that it is wrong and I give them to You.

"From now on, if You want me to eat any of Your pineapples, fine. You just go right ahead and give them to us. If not, fine. It doesn't really matter."

So I gave them to God, and the natives stole the pineapples as usual.

I thought to myself, "See, God, You can't control them either."

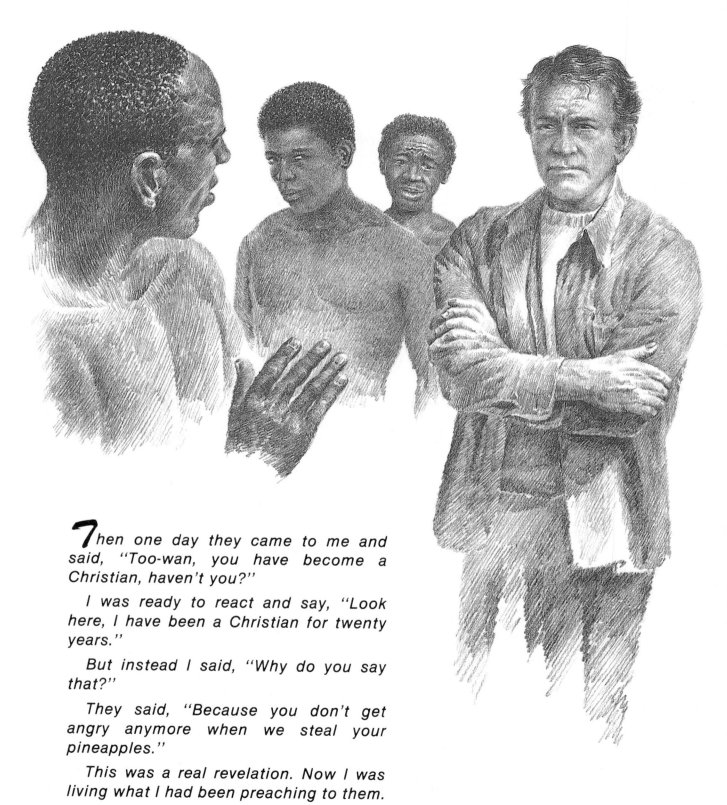

*7*hen one day they came to me and said, "Too-wan, you have become a Christian, haven't you?"

I was ready to react and say, "Look here, I have been a Christian for twenty years."

But instead I said, "Why do you say that?"

They said, "Because you don't get angry anymore when we steal your pineapples."

This was a real revelation. Now I was living what I had been preaching to them.

I had been telling them to love one another, be kind to one another, and I had always been standing up for my rights, and they knew it.

Finally, one bright lad started thinking and said, "Now, why don't you get angry anymore?"

I said, "I have given that garden away. It isn't my garden anymore. So you are not stealing my pineapples. I don't have to get angry anymore."

Another guy started to think even more and he said, "Who did you give that garden to?"

They looked around. "Did he give it to you?" "Did he give it to you?" "Whose is it anyway?"

"Whose pineapples are we stealing?"

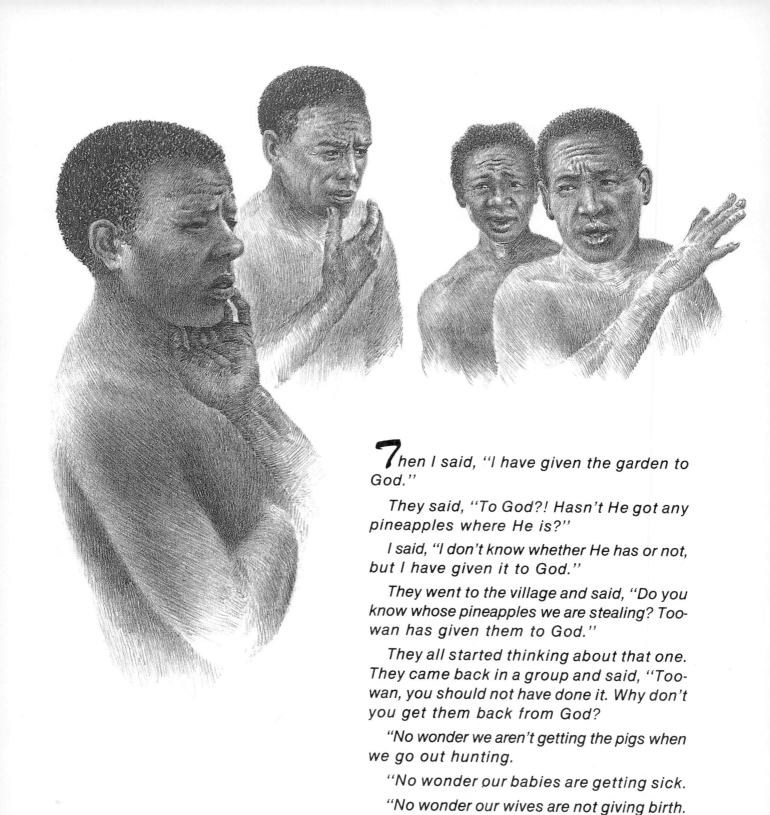

*7*hen I said, "I have given the garden to God."

They said, "To God?! Hasn't He got any pineapples where He is?"

I said, "I don't know whether He has or not, but I have given it to God."

They went to the village and said, "Do you know whose pineapples we are stealing? Too-wan has given them to God."

They all started thinking about that one. They came back in a group and said, "Too-wan, you should not have done it. Why don't you get them back from God?

"No wonder we aren't getting the pigs when we go out hunting.

"No wonder our babies are getting sick.

"No wonder our wives are not giving birth.

"No wonder the fish aren't biting."

Then they said, "We shouldn't steal them anymore if they are God's, should we?"

7hey were afraid of God.

So then the pineapples began to ripen. The natives came and said, "Too-wan, your pineapples are ripe."

I said, "They are not mine. They belong to God."

They said, "But they are going to get rotten. You had better pick them."

And so, I got some and I let the natives take some.

When my family sat down to eat them, I said, "Lord, we are eating Your pineapples. Thank You for giving them to us."

All those years those natives were watching me and listening to my words. They saw that the two didn't match. But when I began to change, they did too.

Soon many natives decided to become Christians.

7he principle of giving to God was really working. I could hardly believe it myself. I started giving other things to God.

One day my son was near death and there was no way to get him to a doctor. I suddenly realized that I'd never given my son to God! So I prayed, "God, I give my son to You. Whatever You want to do is fine."

That was harder than giving God the pineapple garden!

I was prepared for God to take my son. But that night the fever broke, and my son got well.

7he natives began bringing things for me to fix.

I said, "God, my time is Yours. If You want me to fix harmonicas and pots and shovels out here on the mission field, fine!"

I wasn't getting as much Bible translation done, but more and more people were being won to Christ.

They kept saying, "Too-wan has become a Christian. He tells us to love one another and now he is starting to love us."

One day I was fixing a broken chair. A native saw me and said, "Here, let me help you hold it."

After we fixed it I said, "Well, aren't you going to ask me for any salt?"

He said, "No, Too-wan. Don't you remember? You helped me fix my shovel. Now I help you fix your chair."

I thought, "Man! That is the first time they did anything for me without getting paid for it."

7hen one day I saw something in the Bible. I had never noticed it before.

"And when ye shall come into the land, and shall have planted all manner of trees for food, . . . three years shall it be as uncircumcised unto you; it shall not be eaten of. But in the fourth year all the fruit thereof shall be holy with which to praise the Lord. And in the fifth year shall ye eat of the fruit thereof, that it may yield unto you the increase thereof: I am the Lord your God." Leviticus 19:23-25

7inally I understood!

God never intended me to eat those pineapples the first year they were ripe! He wanted me to dedicate them to Him. Then He wanted me to give them to the natives so that they could see my good works and glorify my Father Who was in heaven. If I had only done this, the natives would have urged me to eat the pineapples the fifth year.

Man! All the trouble I could have avoided!

WHAT IS YOUR "PINEAPPLE GARDEN"?

HOW TO GIVE YOUR PINEAPPLE GARDEN TO GOD

1. RECALL WHAT MAKES YOU ANGRY

The missionary was angry with the natives for eating his pineapples. Maybe you get angry with your parents for not respecting your opinions, or approving of your activities, or accepting the one you want to date. Perhaps you get angry with friends for saying things about you that aren't true or for excluding you from their activities. You might even get angry at God for making you with a physical handicap or putting you in a family that doesn't show love for each other.

2. LIST YOUR RIGHTS WHICH OTHERS ARE VIOLATING

The natives weren't respecting the missionary's right to eat his own pineapples. Maybe your parents aren't respecting the rights that you have to your own opinions, planning your own activities, or choosing your own friends. Perhaps your friends don't respect your right to a good reputation or to participate in their activities. You may even feel that God is denying your right to enjoy health and a happy family.

3. TRANSFER YOUR RIGHTS TO GOD

Picture yourself kneeling in the presence of God and putting all of your rights on His altar. Then bow your head and tell God that you are giving them all to Him. He can do with them whatever He wants. This means you don't have any more rights to your own plans, or will, or possessions, or friends, or opinions, or reputation. All your rights belong to God.

4. PURPOSE TO THANK GOD WHATEVER HAPPENS

God may see that some of the rights that you gave to Him would be very harmful for your spiritual growth. He will withhold these from you and you can thank Him for it. Other rights may be loaned back to you. For these you can also thank God. Now they are not rights. They are privileges to be used for God's purpose.

5. USE FUTURE ANGER AS GOD'S ALARM SYSTEM

When we give all of our rights to God, we are demonstrating the quality of meekness. Meekness is yielding our rights to God. It is just the opposite of anger. Anger occurs when we demand our own rights. In fact, whenever we get angry it is a signal that somebody has discovered one of our rights that we have not yet given to God. Because of this, we can use anger as an alarm system to search out rights and transfer them to God.

When we follow these steps, we are obeying the instruction of Jesus. "If any man will come after me, let him deny himself, and take up his cross daily, and follow me. For whosoever will save his life will lose it, but whosoever shall lose his life for My sake, shall save it. For what is a man advantaged if he gain the whole world and lose himself or be cast away." (Luke 9:23-25)

LET THIS MIND BE IN YOU
WHICH WAS IN CHRIST JESUS ...

The principle of yielding rights is demonstrated by the Lord Jesus Christ when He, Who was God, did not cling to His rights as God's equal, but set aside His rights and took upon Himself the position of a servant. He lived a life of total obedience, even to dying on the cross for our sin.

Because of this, God has highly exalted Him and given Him a name that is above every name, that at the name of Jesus every knee should bow and every tongue should confess that Jesus Christ is Lord. (Philippians 2:5-11)